THE ART OF YURI GORBACHEV

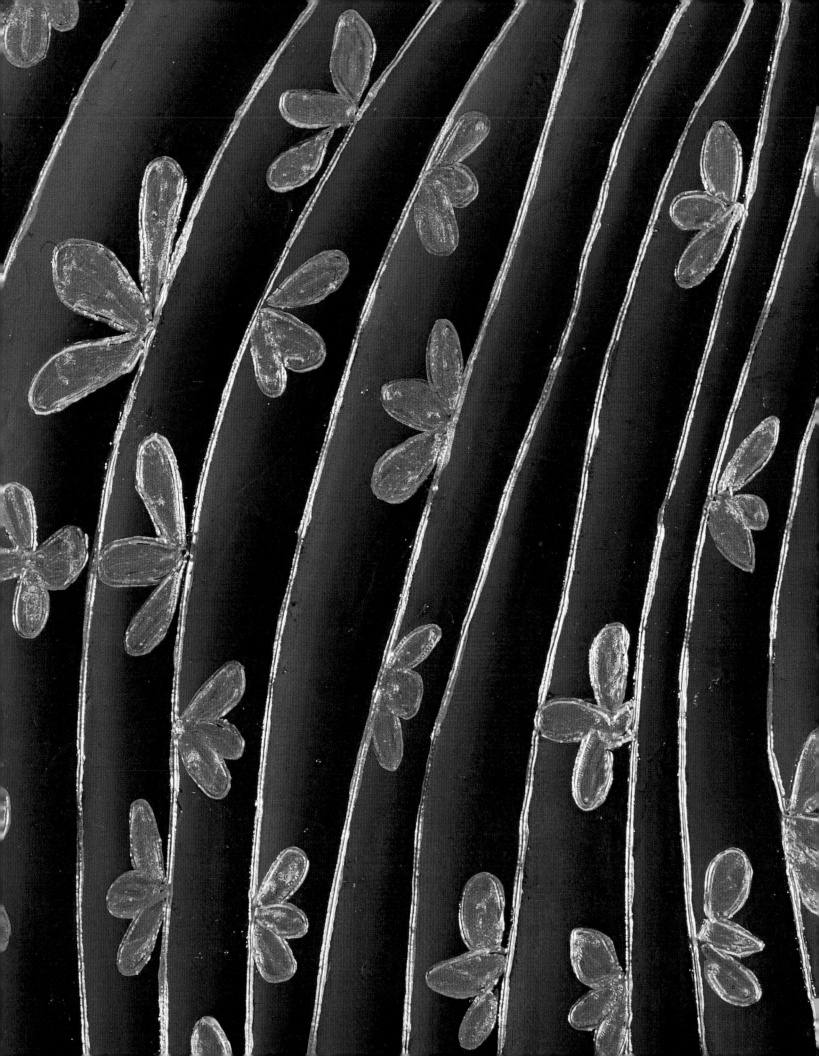

THE ART OF
YURI GORBACHEV

Introduction by Yaroslav Mogutin

Essay by Carey Goldberg

RIZZOLI
NEW YORK

ACKNOWLEDGMENTS

My warmest thanks to the people who inspired me and helped make this book possible: Beatrice Booth, Nina Gavrilova, Adrienne Adler, Alexander Zakharov, Natasha Bozarnachuk, Alexander Tchoulkov, and Platon, Ilia, and Mikhail Gorbachev, my sons.

And special thanks to my editor, Megan McFarland, and book designers, Patrick Seymour and Vivien Sung.

— Yuri Gorbachev

International Art Publishers gratefully acknowledges the collaboration of Don Nay, Dana A. Yarger, and Megan McFarland.

First published in the United States of America in 1998 by
Rizzoli International Publications, Inc.
300 Park Avenue South, New York NY 10010

INTERNATIONAL ART PUBLISHERS IS THE WORLDWIDE EXCLUSIVE AGENT FOR THE ARTWORK OF YURI GORBACHEV. FOR ARTWORK AND EXHIBITION INQUIRIES, CALL 800 388 1358.

Library of Congress Cataloging-in-Publication Data

Gorbachev, Yuri.
The Art of Yuri Gorbachev / introduction by Yaroslav Mogutin;
essay by Carey Goldberg.
p.   cm.
ISBN 0–8478–2143–9
1. Gorbachev, Yuri – Catalogs. I. Goldberg, Carey. II. Title
ND699.G6385A4 1998   98 – 7653
759.7 – dc21   CIP

ARTWORK PHOTOGRAPHED BY PETER GRITSYK.

Endpapers: Original design, 1998.
Frontispiece: Detail, CZAR NIKOLAI AND HIS WIFE. 30 x 40 inches, 1994.
p. 6: Detail, ANGEL. 22 x 26 inches, 1982.
p. 20: Detail, SLEEPING ANGEL. 50 x 66 inches, 1992.
p. 36: Detail, HORSES NEAR MY LAKE. 30 x 40 inches, 1998.
p. 60: Detail, CLOWN WITH LION. 30 x 40 inches, 1996.
p. 70: Detail, LANDSCAPE WITH RICE FIELDS IN BALI, 50 x 66 inches, 1996.
p. 82: Detail, CSAR NIKOLAI AND HIS WIFE. 30 x 40 inches, 1994.
p. 96: Detail, DEATH OF BELIEVER, DEATH OF SINNER, 30 x 40 inches, 1997.
p. 118: Detail, FOUR ELEMENTS: EARTH, 24 x 48 inches, 1998.
p. 136: Detail, STOLICHNAYA HOLIDAY PAINTING. 36 x 48 inches, 1995.

Designed by Tsang Seymour Design
Printed and bound in Italy

Contents

By Yaroslav Mogutin

Paradise Lost and Regained:

The Jester's Art of Yuri Gorbachev

Yuri Gorbachev came to New York at the most inauspicious of times. In 1991, the concentration of Russian artists on the American and, more broadly, the Western art markets passed all reasonable bounds. Competition was intense, and the supply of Russian art far exceeded demand.

Cold-war times had passed for good and neither ideology nor dissent was being sold or bought any longer. Dissidents' tears no longer tugged at one's heartstrings. Gone, too, were post-perestroika euphoria and the concomitant unprecedented burst of popular interest in all things Soviet and Russian. But political and ideological fashions were not all that had changed. There were also new trends in contemporary art. Even the most successful Russian conceptualist artists were no longer being bought, much less the dinosaurs of Soviet unofficial art of the 1950s and 1960s (those whom the comic party chief Khrushchev angrily, but with unexpected accuracy, called "abstractionists and pederasts"). The dust had settled, and the contemporary Soviet avant-garde, which has always been considered kitschy and exotic, found itself relegated once more to its narrow corner of the art world.

In spite of – or, more accurately, thanks to – all this, the year 1991, marked by Mikhail Gorbachev's precipitous fall from Russia's political Olympus, saw Yuri Gorbachev's rapid ascent to the Olympus of the Western art world. The reasons for his success can be found in all those things that distinguish him from the mass of Russian artists in the West.

Yuri Gorbachev in his ceramics studio in Odessa, c.1987.

First and foremost, his legend and his image have played a decisive role in Gorbachev's success. Here is a man with no worries – from RUSSIA? Could that be? Before Gorbachev, such a thing was almost impossible to believe. And it didn't matter exactly what sort of worries one had in mind – political or personal, rare or commonplace. Neither dissident, politician, instigator, scandalmonger, schemer, snob, nor poseur; never convicted, either as a parasite on the body politic or for anti-Soviet activity; never struggled against the accursed Communist regime; never confined to a labor camp; never incarcerated in a sanitarium; never the object of KGB curiosity; never brawled with the cops; never lay with his paintings in the bulldozers' path; never organized underground showings, seeing as he suffered no lack of legal exhibitions – it was hardly even scary to deal with such a Russian!

Unlike the majority of Russian artists who left for the West during the "stagnation" era of the 1970s and post-perestroika in the 1980s, Gorbachev was never an outsider, either by design or by circumstance. He made a name for himself while still in Russia – by his art, and not by conflict with the authorities.

Gorbachev's image is the antithesis of the stereotypical, caricatured Russians that Americans had seen in the cheap propaganda films of the cold-war period. Energetic, gregarious, and charming, Gorbachev is for Americans the personification of the celebrated great big Russian soul in a great big Russian body. His personality wins people over before they even see his work. It is not surprising that the press has taken to him, drawn by a charisma that cannot be acquired or imitated, for one either has charisma or one does not and never will.

And, of course, there is his name, which due to circumstances beyond Yuri's control has become one of those few difficult-to-pronounce Russian names that foreigners have memorized thoroughly. But he neither chose nor concocted the name – he was simply born with it! If one were to list luck among the keys to Gorbachev's success, this would be where that luck both begins and ends, for he possesses all the qualities that might be required of him beyond luck – talent, originality, and the ability to show that he is not merely worthy of his great name, but merits serious interest on his own terms.

Devotees who speak with Yuri find themselves convinced that his paintings are charged with a certain positive and life-affirming "joyous" energy. His is an art that flows from within, from the memories, sensations, impulses, and power in the human subconscious.

Gorbachev's artistic world is woven from legends, fairy-tales, and folk images, half dream and half reality. This world is always gentle, harmonious, and beautiful, whatever the images and stories one chooses to take from it: idyllic landscapes with churches and towers; vivid still lifes with fruit, flowers, a parrot; woodcuts of erotic or playfully rude scenes; clashes between various mythological creatures; portraits of the artist's ancestors or neighbors from the village of his childhood, portraits no less radiant and opulent than those of the czar's family or the Russian Orthodox icons that "come alive" for Gorbachev; plump Russian bathing beauties; or popular holiday feasts and festivals.

This Russia cannot be seen on a newscast or in films, you will not read about it in the newspapers, you won't be told of it by émigré Russians, nor will you find it in the paintings of Russian artists in the West. This Russia, which, like the legendary invisible city of Kitezh, reveals itself only to a chosen few, is kept in the genetic memory of a people and is passed from one generation to the next in the oral tradition of folklore and legends. In the best of Gorbachev's works are found not only the marks of a thousand years of Orthodox history and culture, but also certain profound, pre-Christian, pagan layers of the Russian national consciousness.

Gorbachev's genuine "Russianness," the foundation of his work, has none of the aggressive and hysterical angst and pathos so characteristic of certain other Russian artists who have used folk themes as an object for nationalistic speculation. While remaining a patriotic Russian and taking pride in his heritage, Yuri espouses cosmopolitan views, combining in his paintings elements from various cultures. It is precisely this quality that makes Gorbachev's work so attractive to people of the disparate countries where it has been exhibited.

It is instructive to note that the most productive period of Gorbachev's career, which is marked by a particularly spirited and vivid palette, began with his move to New York, when nostalgia was transformed in a kaleidoscope of picturesque Russian images. There is a touching naïveté and an almost childlike innocence in many of his works, and one can hardly miss an exalted and blissful nostalgia for the lost paradise of youth. Yuri's own boyhood could hardly be called cloudless or uncomplicated; nevertheless, it has become for him a major inspiration, an endless source of themes and images.

In 1995, Gorbachev suddenly found his lost paradise – not in his native Russia, but in Bali. His studio was transformed into a museum where Indonesian masks, statues, rugs, and other decorative objects crowded aside Russian icons. The impact of his encounter with this hitherto unfamiliar culture was

9

Studies for Balinese
Icon Series
9.5 x 11 inches, 1996
Ink, color pencil, and
gold pen

Yuri Gorbachev with his mother, Nina, 1949.

so strong that Indonesian motifs became central to his work. A certain logic can be perceived in the effortless flow of Indonesian art into Gorbachev's creations, a certain inherent commonality of color schemes and attitudes.

"I have always enjoyed bringing surprise and amusement to people!" Yuri states. Thanks to this ability, in his childhood he became everyone's darling in Uglovka, his native village not far from the old city of Novgorod. The visit of a photographer from the city was a historic event there. The entire population of Uglovka, dressed up as for a holiday, waited in line to be captured in a photograph. Solemn and mysterious, the photographer would disappear under the black fabric behind the camera, and the magic would happen. That very moment of disappearing under the black cloth was the most exciting and intriguing part for little Yuri. When the photographer left, Yuri decided to repeat the magic on his own. It was the first manifestation of his artistic talents. Having made something remotely resembling a camera out of a porridge box and a piece of black fabric, he started offering his services to his neighbors. Finding a customer, Yuri would disappear under the black fabric and rapidly draw a small portrait "photograph." In that postwar time pencils were hard to come by, so he would draw with thin pieces of coal. Of course, his "photographs" were not as good as those of the city photographer, but there was no end of people wanting to sit for his small pictures. He became a local celebrity. Everyone invited him to be their guest, treated him with food, wanted to be friends with him — until someone found out that his pictures were not real. The forgery was revealed, but people had no wish to say good-bye to his "photos." Gorbachev the artist had achieved his first success. He was only six then.

Gorbachev's ability to surprise and amuse people has developed through the years of his artistic career. Using sometimes the simplest subjects for his paintings, he transforms them until they acquire their special, Gorbachev-style uniqueness. In a snowy Russian landscape with beautiful churches, flowers blossom in the background, or a still life with exotic fruits and a parrot is disturbed by a racing troika. Each is like a picture within a picture.

All Gorbachev's works vibrate with a theatrical or carnival quality. They reflect the rich Russian culture of the grotesque, of folk humor, of street fairs with a Punch-and-Judy show and clowns in colorful costumes. Explaining why the circus became one of his favorite subjects, Gorbachev recalls the strong impression made on him during his Uglovka childhood by the visit of a traveling circus: "It was like the arrival of a UFO full of aliens!"

Yuri's mother became a victim of Stalinist repression. She was thrown into jail where, together with the other prisoners, she tailored costumes for puppets and clowns. In the postwar years there was a shortage of clothing, so Yuri was especially proud walking around Uglovka wearing clown pants sent to him by his mother. "Everybody had gray, gloomy clothes, and I had those loud pants made from checked material!" he recalls. "I liked them so much that I carried through my entire life that impression of a holiday from those clown costumes. Even in my adult age I preferred bright clothes and was always

Studies for Czar Series
9.5 x 11 inches, 1996
Ink, color pencil, and
gold pen

wearing checked shorts, trousers, and jackets until I was in my thirties." Now, as a contrast to the brightness of his paintings, Gorbachev prefers a pointedly serious and strict style, wearing all black. "Maybe it's some sort of compensation for my wild youth!" he says laughing.

Russian history has always been an inspiration for Gorbachev. His series of portraits of the Romanov czars and czarinas is an unprecedented attempt to create a gallery of images of all eighteen members of this famous and influential dynasty, which lasted more than three centuries. The portraits of the last czar, Nicholas II, and his family have a special place in this series. They reflect not only the interest in this controversial figure in the West, but also the new attitudes toward his murder by the Bolsheviks. In Gorbachev's interpretation, the images of Csar Nicholas have neither tragic character nor martyr's aura. They are informal portraits of a celebrity rather than of a tyrant-autocrat, without the usual historical and ideological context. "When I started working on this series, I was thinking of czars as simple people," Yuri explains. "I wanted to show them as common individuals with their weaknesses and defects. I created a special costume for each of them. For me it was like a Russian puppet show of some sort. I was dressing czars like puppets."

Turning to religious motifs, Gorbachev created a series of works that build upon the ancient Russian tradition of icon painting. It should be noted that his native region of Novgorod gave to the world one of the great schools of icon painting, founded by Andrei Rublyov (ca. 1360 – ca. 1430), a student of the famous Byzantine painter Feofan the Greek. Gorbachev considers Rublyov, who was recently proclaimed a saint by the Russian Orthodox Church, one of his most important teachers in painting, along with Picasso, Rousseau, Kandinsky, and Malevich.

"Icons surrounded me from the very moment of my birth," Gorbachev says. "My first memories are of icons at my grandmother's home. They occupied

Yuri Gorbachev and
grandmother Natalya
in Russia, c. 1954.

the most important spot in the house. Saint George, Mary with the Child, the Holy Trinity, and others – they were like real people for me. For many simple people in pre-Revolutionary Russia, icons were the only source of culture and knowledge, a replacement for art, literature, and theater. In the villages there were at least three icons in every house.

"Unfortunately, the Western audience often is not prepared for a clear perception of Byzantine and Russian icons. For many Westerners icons are like MATRYOSHKAS [sets of nesting dolls]. I saw how crowds of people were waiting in line for three hours to get into the Byzantine show at the Metropolitan Museum of Art and then, after getting in with such effort, they would quickly get tired before even finishing the viewing. My main goal is to explain to them the beauty of Russian icons. My icons bring people a holiday."

Gorbachev's icons of the most respected Russian saints and martyrs, the Holy Trinity, the Virgin Mary, and Jesus Christ, give Western viewers an opportunity to take a new look at classical Orthodox images, which become more contemporary, secular, and understandable in his interpretation. Unlike traditional Orthodox icons, often painted in depressingly dark tones, Gorbachev's icons are full of bright colors, sunshine, and positive energy. They can easily be imagined in any modern interior. Even Gorbachev's Last Judgment does not seem that frightening, and his sinners accept hell's tortures with joyful expressions on their faces. The themes of celebration and the grotesque are still the most important ones for the artist.

Evolution is the theme of a new phase in the artist's work. Before entering this phase, Gorbachev, who has a degree in philosophy from Leningrad State University, had devoted himself primarily to the "philosophy of life," finding meaning, beauty, and harmony in the most simple and seemingly primitive things of his surroundings. In his series of works on the development of different forms of life on Earth, for the first time in his art, Gorbachev's philosophical education and his life philosophy converge. "I wanted to tell my audience about serious philosophical things without pretentiousness and snobbishness, by using the simple and understandable language of figurative art. I hate snobbishness! I think it's the worst human quality there is. I tried to illustrate an age-old philosophical argument about the primacy of the material world and consciousness, the Darwinian theory and the history of evolution, beginning with the most primitive forms of life up to the appearance of the first human beings, Adam and Eve. I tried to do it that way so it would be interesting and understandable for everybody, both adults and kids."

As Gorbachev began to choose subjects that were more and more sophisticated, he was developing his technique as well. Prior to starting his career as a painter, he spent more than twenty years as a ceramic artist. According to Yuri, it was great training for him: "It's not enough to have strong hands to become a real master of ceramics. You also need rich fantasy and emotional character in order to have the subject and the image of your future work in your head before the clay dries and becomes hard. Strict central composition was always important for my art."

Gorbachev's technique is unique. First, he uses a special knife to apply to the canvas a thick coat of oil paint of a neutral color. Then, carefully, trying not to damage the texture, he makes deep lines with quick and precise movements of a metal stick. After this step he waits about two weeks for the paint to dry. At this point he begins the major portion of the work. The contours of the image being ready, he applies three or four coats of oil paint until the desired intensity of color is reached. Gorbachev says that he does not like acrylic paint because it does not have such natural nuances and dries too fast, whereas oil paint is "stretchy" and allows a more plastic image. Special lacquer used by Gorbachev contains more then twenty different elements. The recipe for the lacquer is one of the artist's secrets. A finished work is covered with a thick coat of the lacquer, which makes the colors brighter and brings them more into contrast.

Gilding is the last phase of the work. Inspired by magnificent Byzantine art and by the works of Peter Carl Fabergé, Gorbachev uses gold, silver, and bronze extensively in his paintings. The metals highlight the composition, adding distinctness and brightness to his colors, as well as an impression of old-style nobility.

Before Gorbachev came on the scene, Russian émigré art seemed to be permeated by a strained seriousness, preoccupied with its own obsessions and complexes, bent on masochistically worrying old wounds and sores, fixated on an accursed Soviet past and on other troubles and crises – all of which could offer Western audiences only depression and melancholy. In contrast, Gorbachev took up in his works the role of the wandering minstrel-fool of Russian folklore, preferring to entertain and amuse rather than annoy and frighten. (It is no coincidence that the circus and the clown are among his most beloved themes.) Is it surprising that the public found his approach much more to its taste?

"Yuri, why is it that in your landscapes the wind blows one way, but the trees bend in the other?" I asked. "So my trees are crazy," laughed Gorbachev. In his works, you will always find humor and that joyous, positive energy that he has taken from a certain abstract and difficult-to-define concept and turned into a factor in his artistic achievements.

Translated from the Russian by John William Narins and the author.

13

By Carey Goldberg

The Other Gorbachev

The first time I met Yuri Gorbachev, to interview him for THE NEW YORK TIMES, he hoisted up his brightly patterned shirt to show me that, unlike his cold-war-busting cousin, Mikhail S. Gorbachev, this Gorbachev had had his birthmark removed. There it was, a nicely healing scar under his arm, left by a good American surgeon. And there you have it, a first impression of a successful artist who is so delightfully loose, so gleefully childlike, that he can happily bare his armpit to THE NEW YORK TIMES.

After that, the impressions only got brighter. There is no better interview subject than a man who just wants to make people happy, a man so brimming with energy that he repeats and re-repeats words for emphasis, a man with a mission so simple and sweet that it works for Americans and Russians and Indonesians alike. And there is no better art, to my taste, than art that radiates the same kind of joie de vivre so that it acts as a tonic on all those who see it, uplifting not only with its beauty but with an exuberance as potent as the frantic blooming of northern plants in summer.

"I have to make people happy," "Yuri says (often). "It sounds banal, but it's energy, this positive energy, that frees people and has no pretensions." That Gorbachev energy works. At an ArtExpo fair in Manhattan, browsers could be seen breaking into smiles as they passed Yuri's glowing, gilded paintings — the kind of smiles that come as a reflex when you step out of a cool, dim house into heavenly sunshine.

A longtime friend of Yuri's, Natasha Gotsouliak, said she uses his paintings in her work as a psychologist, hanging them in the "recharge room." She has found that they have an uplifting effect on chronically depressed patients. "Yuri's energy is very optimistic, and his paintings mirror his energy," she said.

Yuri Gorbachev in his
studio, New York, 1997.

"He's very giving, and that's why he's never depressed. He knows that to be happy, you have to share."

It is one of Yuri's mantras that he is not "Russian Russian Russian," and there is no question that his art is truly international, becoming more so every day as he ventures into new cultural hybrids. But it is striking nonetheless that Russia could be the birthplace of such an anomalous little beacon of joy — Russia, the land so expert in misery that its global karma, some Russians say, is to show the rest of the world how not to do things. So upbeat is Yuri that he manages to turn even a portrait of Czar Nicholas II and his family — an ensemble of martyrs doomed to be slaughtered by Bolsheviks in a Yekaterinburg cellar in 1918 — into a pleasant picture with a lambent holiday atmosphere. He performs the same happy-making magic with devils and depictions of hell. (He does not want people to be scared of hell because then they will be even more afraid to die, he says.) His versions of Russian icons turn those solemn-eyed Byzantine portraits into lilting and shining contemporary delights, and his still lifes turn bouquets of flowers into exploding fireworks of color. "Life is short, and I want to make people happy," he says (often).

Some of his works are reminiscent of Fabergé eggs, not only in their technique but in the sense they convey of a precious treasure, painstaking in its creation and yet so brazenly calculated to please that it will enrapture even a child. Others bring you into a fabulous, Chagall-like world where gravity has been cancelled, animals fix you with loving human eyes, women are plump and irresistible as dumplings, and winter means joy and flowers and sparkles. All, with almost no exception, make you feel good.

There is a possible psychological explanation for Yuri's drive to please. In his childhood, he says, growing up in a small village near Novgorod in northwestern Russia, he came to feel responsible for keeping his family happy while his mother was in a Soviet prison. There are possible economic explanations as well. Gloom, Yuri admits easily, doesn't sell: "When other Russian artists ask me why they don't have more success, I say, 'Enough of this black negative energy. Americans don't want that. People are tired of it. Why not do something original? Maybe someone will even buy something from you.'"

This is my own favorite theory about the force of nature that is Yuri Gorbachev: So many Russians have been stunted by history, by climate, by diet, by the Russian imprecation not to "stick out," not to be the daisy whose head sticks up farther than the others and is therefore first to be picked. But every once in a while, along comes one who is by nature so strong, so talented, so good, and so lucky that he is never ground up by the millstone of Russian existence; he is an example of how the classically Russian desire to "embrace the world" can develop when it survives the system unscathed.

Here, though, is one of the most interesting twists of Yuri's career. It makes sense that he developed such an aversion to all that is black and gloomy because he lived, until 1991, in a country where those were the dominant hues (aside from red). But the fascinating surprise is that after he immigrated, something in him responded to Americans — and their problems that became

RAM AND BIRD
ON COW
18 inches (height),
1980
Stoneware, endobe,
enamel, and glaze

visible only at close range – with an even more powerful urge to cheer, and his work became even brighter. "Before I moved to America, I thought everyone in America was lucky and happy," he said. "I never thought my colors would become more bright here. But I would like to make the American people very happy. This is my idea."

There is nothing of the factory painter about Yuri. His artistic explorations involve risks that have little to do with the bottom line – as witness his astounding foray into Indonesian art and culture, the adoption of a country (and its adoption of him) purely on the basis of some spiritual kindredness. The Indonesian people, Yuri says, are like flowers. He has come to spend two months a year on Bali, and the Indonesian influence has penetrated his life, from the batik scarf he often wears to his extensive series on Indonesian themes. "I like mixes, combinations," Yuri says. "I don't like anything in its pure form – it oppresses me."

A preliminary impression of Yuri Gorbachev, formed from his simple words and simply expressed thoughts, may be that he himself is somewhat simple, and his work as well. But that impression would be a mistaken one. Yuri is hampered a bit by language limitations – "My English so disgusting!" he likes to announce – but more often, he uses plain speech because he self-censors, being unwilling to play the more-erudite-than-thou games of the culture world. "I hate snobbish pretensions and boredom. People can be so boring sometimes I want to hit them on the head with a bottle to liven things up!" he jokes.

In fact, Yuri is perfectly comfortable discussing the differences between Democritus and Epicurus, finishing off with a foray into existentialism for good measure, should you stumble into that territory with him. After touring the world for years and meeting the patrons associated with top museums and galleries, he has also developed his own unique analysis of the similarities between the upper classes in countries around the world.

And his work, of course, is not simple at all, despite its naïve style and primitivist look. It includes more than seven hundred signs, a personal alphabet that he has created on the basis of his studies of symbols in a dozen different countries, from China to Russia to Indonesia. For the Chinese, for example, the dragon is the symbol of life; for Americans, the eagle means freedom; and for Russians, the bear means strength and creativity. Then, he says, there are the universal symbols: the sun, moon, and stars or numbers. His works combine those seven hundred symbols in complex interactions, just as musical notes make up complex melodies. For example, he says, an apple in many cultures symbolizes health, long life, and the earth; when Yuri surrounds the apple with a circle, he is symbolizing the protection and long life he wishes for the viewers of his painting. A cat, meaning good luck, combined with three apples – with the number three meaning solidity – implies long-lasting good luck and health. In every picture, there is such a symbolic secret. Every flower, every fish, every animal has meaning in his serigraph series, THE FOUR ELEMENTS. Yuri even spells out the symbols in a brochure: water is "spiritual ideals, purity of soul, spiritual forces flowing through man, fluidity, pleasure." Fire is "the life force within, power, passion, psychic energy, Earth's center, stars, heart of man."

For all its strength, however, Yuri's intellect will never be his dominant trait. His ruling characteristic is, as he might say, energy, energy, energy. As he tells it, his theater career failed miserably because he would get so excited while on stage that he would say his lines before his cue. In this, his seeming to be powered by a supercharged battery, lies his clearest resemblance to the Gorbachev that everyone knows, Mikhail Sergeyevich. When he was leader of the Soviet Union, that Gorbachev used to seem able to perform on the political stage endlessly without flagging, droning on for hours at Party congresses, laughing in the face of jet lag, outlasting negotiators years his junior at summits.

Yuri's grandfather, Fyodor, was the brother of Mikhail's father, Sergei, so that makes them first cousins once removed. They have met several times and exchanged pleasantries, Yuri says, but had no other contact over the years. Owning one of the few Russian names that people all over the world are used to pronouncing has certainly not hurt Yuri. It seems especially natural to see a Gorbachev signature on a Stolichnaya vodka ad — indeed, on anything totemically Russian — and in the collections of the White House, Mikhail Baryshnikov, or Armand Hammer, or among works commissioned by the United Nations for a stamp series on endangered species. Make no mistake about it, Yuri says: the name helped open doors, but nobody buys his paintings for the signature. "People who buy my work don't buy it for the name. I don't think I've been so lucky just because I'm a Gorbachev. I think even if I were named Semyonov, it would be the same." The trick is a troika, he said: "It's not enough to have just a name, or just talent, or just good administration. You have to have all three."

If Yuri's development as an artist continues at its current pace, and if his popularity keeps growing so quickly as well, then, friends joke, someday his cousin Misha may be remembered this way in the history books: "Mikhail Gorbachev — a minor political figure who lived in the era of the artist Yuri Gorbachev."

Based on an article originally published in THE NEW YORK TIMES, August 17, 1995.

Studies for Circus
Series and Animals
9.5 x 11 inches, 1996
Ink, color pencil, and
gold pen

MYTHOLOGICAL, THEATRICAL & HOLIDAY SERIES

NEW KING
50 x 66 inches, 1992
Oil, gold, bronze, and copper on canvas

SLEEPING ANGEL
50 x 66 inches, 1992
Oil, gold, bronze, and copper on canvas

24

THE BATHERS
50 x 66 inches, 1992
Oil, gold, bronze, and copper on canvas

THE MUSICIANS
36 x 48 inches, 1993
Oil, gold, bronze, and copper on canvas

FESTIVAL IN MY CITY
36 x 48 inches, 1993
Oil, gold, bronze, and copper on canvas

28

WOMAN AND THREE STRANGE ANIMALS
50 x 66 inches, 1993
Oil, gold, bronze, and copper on canvas

SUMMER HOLIDAY
66 x 50 inches, 1993
Oil, gold, bronze, and copper on canvas

SHEEP FAMILY
30 x 30 inches, 1994
Oil, gold, bronze, and copper on canvas

THREE WOMEN BATHING
66 x 50 inches, 1993
Oil, gold, bronze, and copper on canvas

DANGEROUS GAME
50 x 66 inches, 1994
Oil, gold, bronze, and copper on canvas

MUSICIAN AND WOMAN WITH BLUE HAIR
40 x 30 inches, 1994
Oil, gold, bronze, and copper on canvas

YURI, BEBE, AND SERGUEI IN PARIS AT THE CHEDIVARS' HOME
48 x 36 inches, 1993
Oil, gold, bronze, and copper on canvas

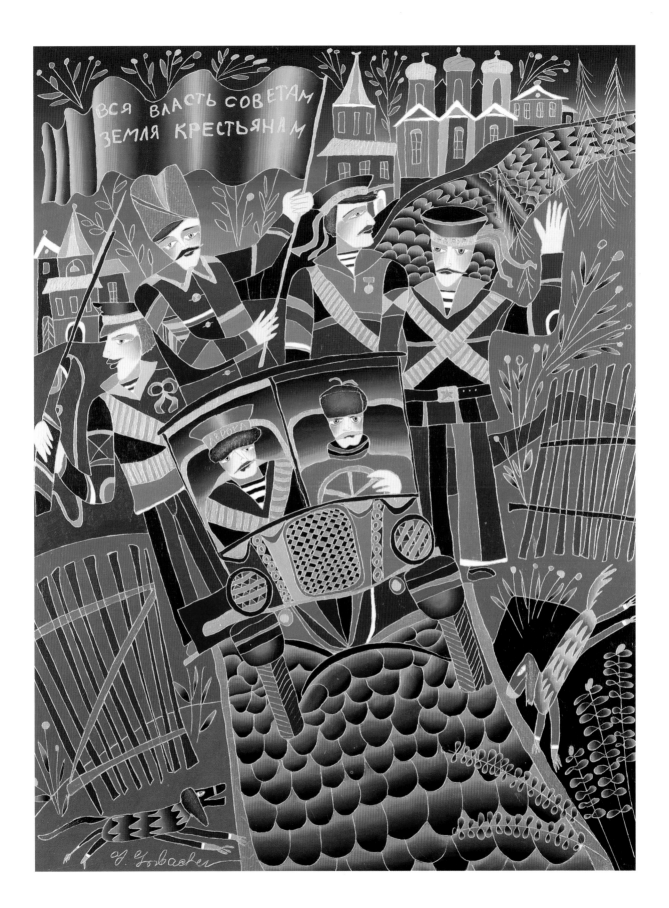

FIRST RUSSIAN DECREE FROM RUSSIAN REVOLUTION
50 x 66 inches, 1994
Oil, gold, bronze, and copper on canvas

2

STILL LIFES, LANDSCAPES & ANIMAL SERIES

SUMMER LANDSCAPE
40 x 30 inches, 1995
Oil, gold, bronze, and copper on canvas

GRAY HORSE
36 x 30 inches, 1995
Oil, gold, bronze, and copper on canvas

OWL IN MY VILLAGE
24 x 30 inches, 1995
Oil, gold, bronze, and copper on canvas

RUNNING HORSES
66 x 50 inches, 1995
Oil, gold, bronze, and copper on canvas

SPRING IN BOROVICHI
60 x 50 inches, 1991
Oil, gold, bronze, and copper on canvas

STILL LIFE WITH BOTTLES
30 x 24 inches, 1995
Oil, gold, bronze, and copper on canvas

STILL LIFE WITH FLOWERS AND WINTER LANDSCAPE
30 x 40 inches, 1996
Oil, gold, bronze, and copper on canvas

STILL LIFE WITH TWO DOGS
40 x 30 inches, 1995
Oil, gold, bronze, and copper on canvas

TROPICAL PARROTS
30 x 40 inches, 1997
Oil, gold, bronze, and copper on canvas

STILL LIFE WITH ROSES
30 x 40 inches, 1997
Oil, gold, bronze, and copper on canvas

AUTUMN IN MY CITY
30 x 30 inches, 1997
Oil, gold, bronze, and copper on canvas

HORSES IN MY VILLAGE
50 x 66 inches, 1997
Oil, gold, bronze, and copper on canvas

FLOWERS AND FRUIT NEAR THE WINDOW
40 x 30 inches, 1998
Oil, gold, bronze, and copper on canvas

STILL LIFE WITH PARROT
30 x 30 inches, 1998
Oil, gold, bronze, and copper on canvas

TROPICAL FISH
40 x 30 inches, 1998
Oil, gold, bronze, and copper on canvas

LAKE IN UGLOVKA
40 x 30 inches, 1998
Oil, gold, bronze, and copper on canvas

STILL LIFE WITH CAT AND PARROT
24 x 30 inches, 1998
Oil, gold, bronze, and copper on canvas

HORSES NEAR MY LAKE
30 x 40 inches, 1998
Oil, gold, bronze, and copper on canvas

3

CIRCUS SERIES

CIRCUS
50 x 66 inches, 1997
Oil, gold, bronze, and copper on canvas

CLOWN ON ROOSTER
30 x 40 inches, 1997
Oil, gold, bronze, and copper on canvas

CLOWN WITH LION
30 x 40 inches, 1996
Oil, gold, bronze, and copper on canvas

CLOWN ON HORSE
36 x 48 inches, 1996
Oil, gold, bronze, and copper on canvas

OLD RUSSIAN CIRCUS
36 x 48 inches, 1996
Oil, gold, bronze, and copper on canvas

CIRCUS RING
36 x 48 inches, 1998
Oil, gold, bronze, and copper on canvas

YURI GORBACHEV WITH BIRDS, SUN, MOON, STARS IN UGLOVKA
30 x 40 inches, 1998
Oil, gold, bronze, and copper on canvas

4

BALINESE ICON SERIES

INDONESIAN CEREMONY
30 x 40 inches, 1995
Oil, gold, bronze, and copper on canvas

MORNING IN BALI
30 x 30 inches, 1996
Oil, gold, bronze, and copper on canvas

BUDDHA
30 x 40 inches, 1996
Oil, gold, bronze, and copper on canvas

MUDRA
50 x 66 inches, 1996
Oil, gold, bronze, and copper on canvas

INDONESIAN PUPPET THEATER
30 x 40 inches, 1996
Oil, gold, bronze, and copper on canvas

LANDSCAPE WITH RICE FIELDS IN BALI
66 x 50 inches, 1996
Oil, gold, bronze, and copper on canvas

BALINESE PRINCESS
36 x 48 inches, 1996
Oil, gold, bronze, and copper on canvas

TRADITIONAL INDONESIAN PLAYING CARDS
40 x 30 inches, 1997
Oil, gold, bronze, and copper on canvas

CZAR SERIES

CZAR NIKOLAI AND HIS WIFE
30 x 40 inches, 1994
Oil, gold, bronze, and copper on canvas

CZAR NIKOLAI AND HIS SON ALEXI
30 x 40 inches. 1995
Oil. gold. bronze. and copper on canvas

86

CZAR NIKOLAI ALEXANDROVICH WITH HIS FAMILY
66 x 50 inches, 1996
Oil, gold, bronze, and copper on canvas

ЦАРЬ

МИХАИЛ ФЕДОРОВИЧ

CZAR MIKHAIL FYODORICH
30 x 40 inches, 1997
Oil, gold, bronze, and copper on canvas

ИМПЕРЕАТРИЦА
ЕКАТЕРИНА ПЕРВАЯ

KATHERINE THE FIRST
30 x 40 inches, 1997
Oil, gold, bronze, and copper on canvas

90

PETER THE GREAT
30 x 40 inches, 1997
Oil, gold, bronze, and copper on canvas

ЦАРИЦА ЕКАТЕРИНА II АЛЕКСЕЕВНА

CATHERINE THE GREAT
30 x 40 inches, 1997
Oil, gold, bronze, and copper on canvas

ROMANOV DYNASTY
50 x 66 inches, 1997
Oil, gold, bronze, and copper on canvas

92

93

CZAR ALEXANDER ALEXANDROVICH
WITH HIS FAMILY
66 x 50 inches, 1997
Oil, gold, bronze, and copper on canvas

ICON SERIES

ST. GEORGE AND THE DRAGON
66 x 74 inches, 1991
Oil, gold, bronze, and copper on canvas

CRUSADER SAINT AND HIS LIFE
50 x 66 inches, 1992
Oil, gold, bronze, and copper on canvas

ST. BORIS AND ST. GLEB
30 x 30 inches, 1996
Oil, gold, bronze, and copper on canvas

CRUCIFIXION
36 x 48 inches, 1995
Oil, gold, bronze, and copper on canvas

ASCENSION
36 x 48 inches, 1997
Oil, gold, bronze, and copper on canvas

104

SEVEN DEADLY SINS
30 x 30 inches, 1996
Oil, gold, bronze, and copper on canvas

PATH TO HELL
30 x 40 inches, 1997
Oil, gold, bronze, and copper on canvas

MADONNA
30 x 30 inches, 1996
Oil, gold, bronze, and copper on canvas

THREE ANGELS
30 x 40 inches, 1994
Oil, gold, bronze, and copper on canvas

TRYPTICH: CHRIST WITH
ST. MICHAEL AND ARCHANGEL GABRIEL
84 x 48 inches, 1996
Oil, gold, bronze, and copper on canvas

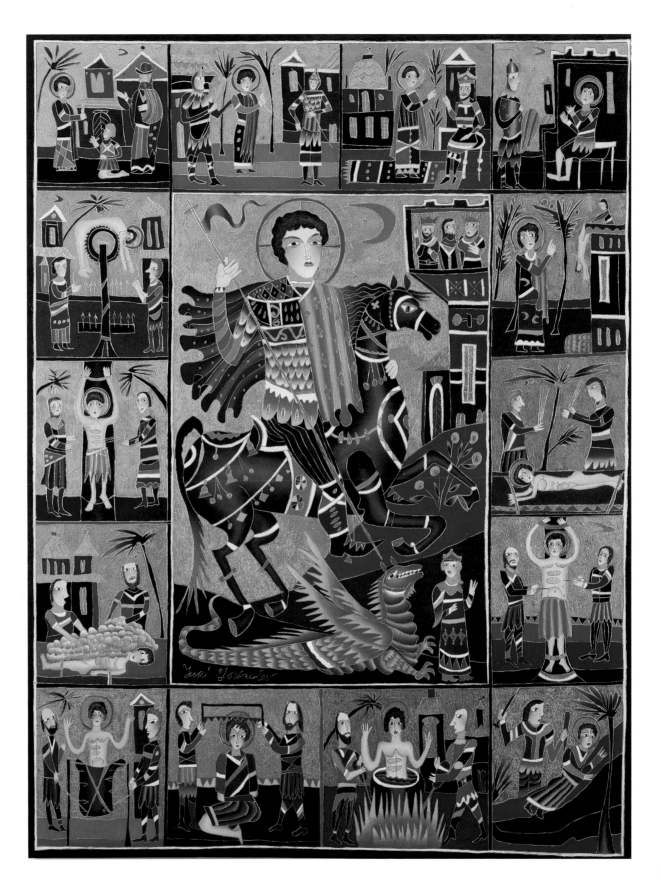

ST. GEORGE AND SCENES FROM HIS LIFE
50 x 66 inches, 1997
Oil, gold, bronze, and copper on canvas

ARCHANGEL MICHAEL
30 x 30 inches, 1997
Oil, gold, bronze, and copper on canvas

DEATH OF BELIEVER, DEATH OF SINNER
30 x 40 inches, 1997
Oil, gold, bronze, and copper on canvas

CHRIST
30 x 30 inches, 1996
Oil, gold, bronze, and copper on canvas

TRYPTICH: MADONNA AND CHILD WITH
ST. GEORGE AND ANGEL OF PROTECTION
84 x 48 inches, 1997
Oil, gold, bronze, and copper on canvas

ADAM AND EVE
66 x 50 inches, 1997
Oil, gold, bronze, and copper on canvas

HELL'S MONSTER WITH SINNER
24 x 24 inches, 1998
Oil, gold, bronze, and copper on canvas

ENOCH'S MOTHER IN HELL
24 x 24 inches, 1998
Oil, gold, bronze, and copper on canvas

ANIMAL FROM HELL
24 x 24 inches, 1998
Oil, gold, bronze, and copper on canvas

BIRD FROM HEAVEN
24 x 24 inches, 1998
Oil, gold, bronze, and copper on canvas

7

EVOLUTION SERIES

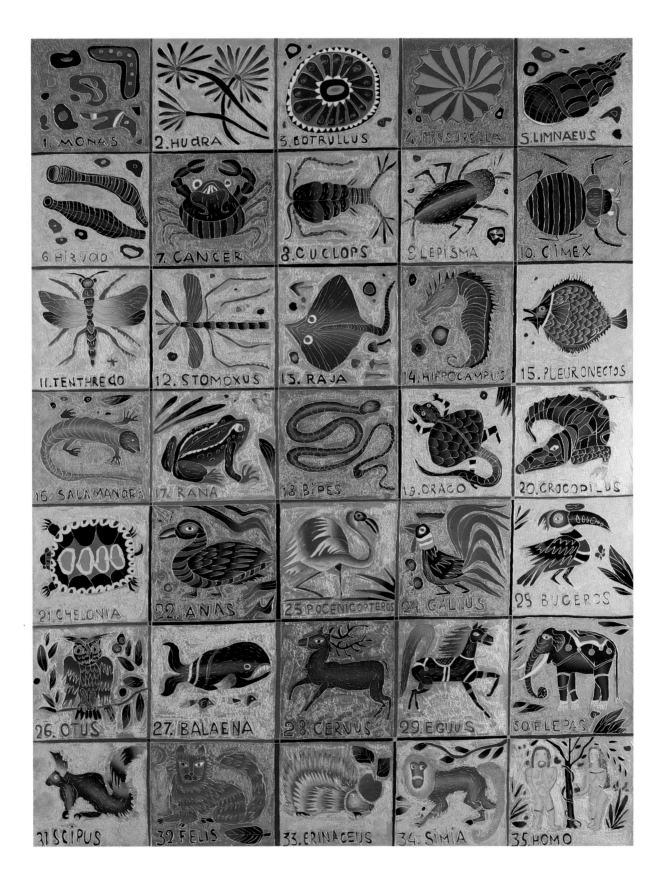

EVOLUTION I
50 x 66 inches, 1998
Oil, gold, bronze, and copper on canvas

AFRICA I
36 x 48 inches, 1997
Oil, gold, bronze, and copper on canvas

BIRDS AND FLOWERS
24 x 24 inches, 1997
Oil, gold, bronze, and copper on canvas

124

SUN
30 x 40 inches, 1998
Oil, gold, bronze, and copper on canvas

COMPOSITION WITH FLOWERS AND FAUNA
30 x 40 inches, 1998
Oil, gold, bronze, and copper on canvas

BIRDS, FISH, AND FLOWERS
36 x 48 inches, 1997
Oil, gold, bronze, and copper on canvas

COMPOSITION WITH TWELVE FLOWERS
40 x 30 inches, 1998
Oil, gold, bronze, and copper on canvas

FOUR ELEMENTS: FIRE
24 x 48 inches, 1998
Oil, gold, bronze, and copper on canvas

FOUR ELEMENTS: EARTH
24 x 48 inches, 1998
Oil, gold, bronze, and copper on canvas

FOUR ELEMENTS: WATER
24 x 48 inches, 1998
Oil, gold, bronze, and copper on canvas

FOUR ELEMENTS: AIR
24 x 48 inches, 1998
Oil, gold, bronze, and copper on canvas

FISH
30 x 30 inches, 1998
Oil, gold, bronze, and copper on canvas

EVOLUTION II: FOUR PAINTINGS
24 x 24 inches each, 1998
Oil, gold, bronze, and copper on canvas

132

1. СТЕБЕЛЬ
2. СИМВОЛИКА
3. ОХОТА
4. ЗВЕРИ
5. БЫК
6. МУЖЧИНА
7. ЦВЕТОК

HUNTER
36 x 48 inches, 1997
Oil, gold, bronze, and copper on canvas

EVOLUTION III
30 x 40 inches, 1998
Oil, gold, bronze, and copper on canvas

EVOLUTION IV
30 x 40 inches, 1998
Oil, gold, bronze, and copper on canvas

GREEN PARROT ON RED FLOWER
9.5 x 12 inches, 1996
Oil, gold, bronze, and copper on canvas

In 1996, the United Nations commissioned Yuri
Gorbachev to create a new painting for the UN
stamp "Endangered Species." Gorbachev presented
this painting, GREEN PARROT ON RED FLOWER,
to UN Secretary-General Boutros Boutros-Ghali
at a preview exhibition in New York in 1996.

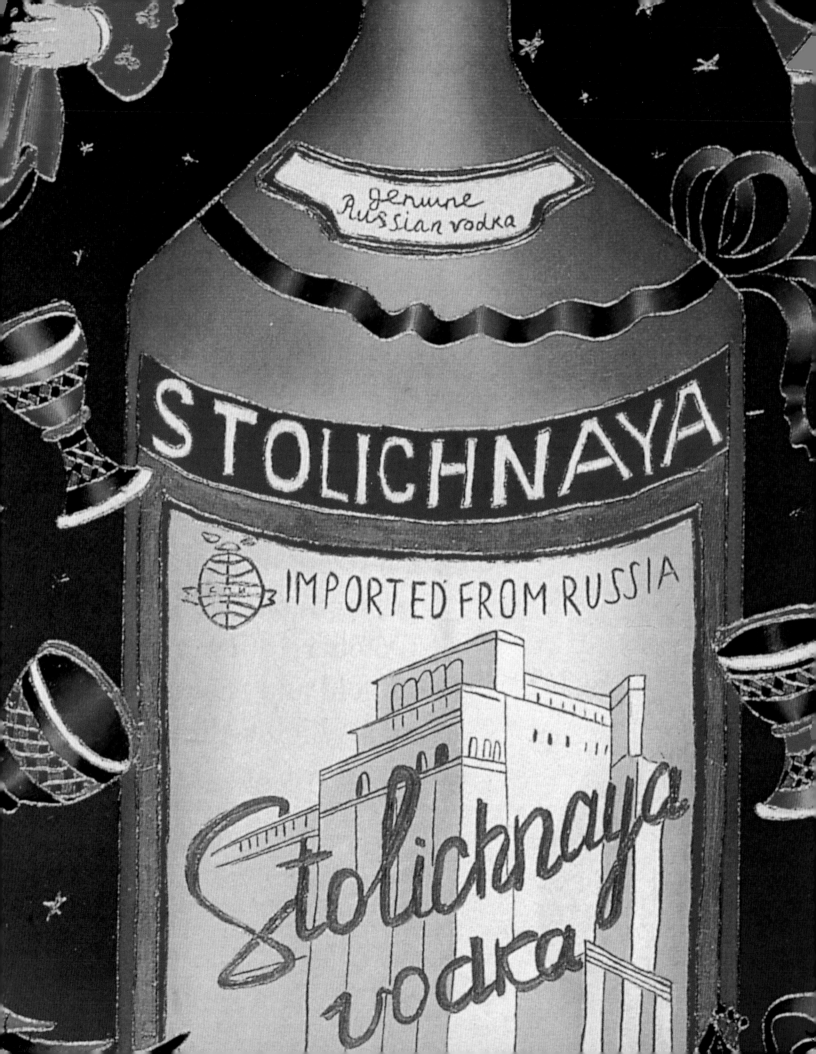

8

STOLICHNAYA HOLIDAY **SERIES**

138

STOLICHNAYA HOLIDAY PAINTINGS
36 x 48 inches each, (left to right) 1994, 1995, 1996, 1997
Oil, gold, bronze, and copper on canvas

My Balinese Icons

I was born in the center of Russia, but over the last few years I have traveled all over the world: Australia, Asia, the Far East, Western Europe, and the United States. Every country has its own strong face, unique culture, tradition, and style. In 1994, when I arrived in Indonesia and Bali for the first time, I felt like I was a witness to one of the wonders of the world. Time stopped for me. Color, sound, day, night, all blended inside me as if I were in a special kind of heaven. I will never forget the beautiful, sensitive Indonesian people with their colorful ceremonies and glorious landscapes, bright birds, and exotic colorful flowers.

Flowers are a very important part of Indonesian and Balinese culture. They are used in all ceremonies: birth, death, and those in between. Flower petals are even used to decorate food and as a motif on frames for paintings. The Balinese people are like flowers themselves, and even their clothes and textiles take the colors and forms of flowers. If you transplant Balinese flowers or birds to another place they will die or lose their color. The people are the same: they couldn't live anywhere else but Bali. That's what makes the island so unique.

I was inspired by every part of Balinese life – dancing, ceremonies, landscapes, people. These mirrored my first impressions of Bali. When I returned to New York, Bali was inside me, and I began to re-create my reflections of this place in my paintings.

— Yuri Gorbachev, February 1998

Yuri Gorbachev in Bali, 1996.

List of Works Illustrated

Chronology

Yuri Gorbachev with
Beatrice Booth and
Alexander Tchoulkov.
New York, 1998.

1948
Born to Mikhail and Nina Gorbachev on
December 29 in Uglovka, near Novgorod,
outside St. Petersburg, the cultural center
of the former USSR.

1952 – 1954
His mother becomes a target of Stalinist
repression and is sent to prison in
Leningrad. Yuri lives with his paternal
grandmother, Natasha Gorbachev, a
colorful, exotic woman.

1954
Yuri's mother is released from prison and
moves in with him and his grandmother.

1956 – 1964
Studies at the Uglovka Public School.
At age 12, wins a competition in
"patriotic art" in the Novgorod Oblast.
Studies ceramics and graduates from
the Borovichi Ceramics Institute in the
Novgorod Oblast.

1968
Works as a technological consultant
at a ceramics factory in Izhevsk, Ural
Region, USSR.

1968 – 1970
Drafted into the regular Russian army,
where he graduates from the School
of Journalism and works as a journalist
for the Byelorussian national army
newspaper.

1971
Attends Leningrad State University, studying in the philosophy department. Works
part-time as a writer and artist for the
magazine of nearby Crosses prison, known
as the "Tsar's Prison," the most infamous
in Russia.

1972
Moves to Odessa, continuing a work-study
program at Leningrad State University.
Begins working with famous ceramic

artists Ivan Gonchorenko and Dina
Kliuvgant. Cultural journalist for GUDOK,
the Moldavian and Ukrainian republic
newspaper. Returns to Leningrad University
periodically for examinations.

1972 – 1977
Exhibits in the USSR, Italy, the United
States, France, Finland, and Czechoslovakia.

1973 – 1977
Attends Odessa State Teachers College,
earning a degree in painting and graphics.

1974 – 1991
Sets up a studio with artist Alexander
Tchoulkov.

1975
Continues studies at Leningrad State
University.

1976
Marries architect Natalya Anichova in
Odessa, with whom he has three sons:
Platon, Ilia, and Mikhail.

1977
Elected member of the prestigious Artist's
Union of the USSR.

1977 – 1987
Exhibits in museums and public spaces
in the USSR. Commissioned to create
several monumental plates for the walls
of hospitals, public halls, and restaurants.
One-man show at the Central House of
Art Workers in Moscow.

1989
Raisa Gorbachev, Secretary of the Soviet
Culture Foundation, organizes Yuri's
one-man show at the foundation's Central
Exhibit Hall.

1990
Solo exhibition in London. First visit to
the United States, where he has three solo
exhibitions in New York.

1991
Close friend Viktor Kovalenka killed during social unrest in Odessa, devastating Yuri. In June, leaves for New York with his family and two artist friends. Decides to remain in the United States when Mikhail Gorbachev is ousted as President of the USSR in August. Meets sculptor Beatrice Booth, who becomes his business manager and close collaborator.

1993
Begins exhibiting throughout the United States. Commissioned as an artist for the Absolut vodka advertising campaign.

1994
Exhibition tour of Asia and Australia. Commissioned to create artwork for Stolichnaya vodka's holiday advertising campaign, continuing through 1997. Moves his studio from Brighton Beach, Brooklyn, to Manhattan.

1995
Spends several months in Bali studying the local culture and traditional art. Travels to Jakarta, Java, Bandung, and other islands of Indonesia. Receives the prize of the Masaryks Academy of Arts in Prague, Czech Republic, and is elected Honorary Member of the academy.

1996
Commissioned by the United Nations to create an original work for a lithograph in conjunction with the release of a UN stamp featuring endangered species. Secretary-General Boutros Boutros-Ghali is presented with the work, GREEN PARROT ON RED FLOWER, at a preview exhibition at the UN in New York. In July, at the opening of the White House Sculpture Exhibit in Washington,D.C., Hillary Rodham Clinton accepts Yuri's work as part of the private collection of President and Mrs. Clinton.

1997
Receives the Franz Kafka Medal for Artistic Merit and Humanism, and an Honorary Diploma from the Masaryks Academy of Art and Culture in Prague, Czech Republic. His monumental painting ST. GEORGE AND THE DRAGON is placed in Vaslov Place, Karuna Passage, Prague, Czech Republic.

1998
His painting HORSES IN MY VILLAGE placed in 5 Penn Plaza, CNN Building, New York. Czar and Icons series begins new exhibition tour.

Yuri Gorbachev
with his sons Mikhail,
Platon, and Ilia.
New York, 1998.

Selected Bibliography

146

Potopov, V.
"Skazka iz Odessa"
(A fairytale from Odessa).
SOVIETSKAYA KULTURA (USSR).
December 4, 1981.

Dirdikina, N.
"Vo Vlastiogny" (In the hands of fire).
MOSKOVSKY KOMSOLMOLETC (USSR).
December 10, 1981.

Yegorova, E.
"Devyetnadzat Noveuch Emien,
Yuri Gorbachev"
(Nineteen new names, Yuri
Gorbachev).
DI SSSR (USSR).
April 1982.

Pridatco, P.
"Sviety Rastvetaut"
(The flowers are blooming).
UKRAINA (USSR).
March 1984.

Saulenko, L.
"Keramica Yuria Gorbacheva"
(Yuri Gorbachev's ceramic art).
DI SSSR (USSR).
November 1984.

YURI GORBACHEV. Catalogue.
Odessa Museum of Western and
Oriental Art (USSR).
1985.

Review of Yuri Gorbachev's
exhibition at the Odessa Museum
of Western and Oriental Art.
ISKUSSTVO (USSR). "Jizn Hudosznikov V
Rosee" (Artistic life in the Soviet Union).
October 1985.

Kuzman, V.
"Mir Keramici" (The world of ceramics).
IZVESTIYA (USSR).
December 5, 1985.

Baranovsky, V.
"Verhom Na Kentavre" (Astride a centaur).
SOVETSKAYA KULTURA (USSR).
December 13, 1986.

Ptitsina, L.
"The Sunny Ceramics Of Yuri
Gorbachev."
ETUDES SOVIETIQUE (France).
July 1986.

Ptitsina, L.
"Solnyitchnaya Keramica"
(Sunny ceramics).
OGONYOK (USSR).
June 1987.

Potapov, V.
"Chudessa Iz Langerona"
(Wonders at Langeron).
SOVETSKAYA KULTURA (USSR).
October 6,1988.

Ilein, Abraham.
"The Message Is More Than the Medium,"
ARTSPEAK.
March 1, 1990.

YURI GORBACHEV PAINTINGS.
Catalogue. London:
Red Square Galleries. 1990.

"Gorbachev à L'Univers des Arts."
MARSEILLES (France).
March 1991.

"Peintures à la russe."
AUBAGNE (France).
March 7, 1991.

Gross, Martha.
"Fisher Island Sustains Coup
by Russian Art."
SUN SENTINEL (Florida).
March 4, 1992.

Moore, Martha T.
"Mother Russia's Red Tag Sale."
USA TODAY.
April 29, 1992.

"Yuri Gorbachev."
NEW YORK POST.
May 1, 1992.

Larkin, Kathy.
"A Palette For Freedom."
DAILY NEWS.
May 12, 1992.

Scaduto, Anthony, Doug Vaughan,
and Linda Stasi.
"State Sides."
NEW YORK NEWSDAY.
May 17, 1992.

"We've Heard That...Yuri Gorbachev."
WASHINGTON POST.
June 1, 1992.

"Gorby Paints Town."
BOSTON GLOBE.
June 6, 1992.

"Personalien p. 246, 247: Yuri
Gorbachev."
DER SPIEGEL (Germany).
June 15, 1992.

Quinn, Michael.
"People: Striking Oil In Brooklyn."
TIME.
June 15, 1992.

"Color, Color, and More Color."
THE WORLD (Vermont).
September 2, 1992.

"Gorbachev and Another Coup."
THE SOUTHAMPTON PRESS
(Southampton, New York).
September 3, 1992.

"The Artist Gorbachev in East
Hampton."
THE EAST HAMPTON STAR
(East Hampton, New York).
September 3, 1992.

YURI GORBACHEV. Catalogue.
Hong Kong: Mimi Ferzt Gallery.
1993.

Mila Andre.
"The World of Art at (Your) Busy Feet."
DAILY NEWS (New York).
February 27, 1994.

"Evening In St. Petersburg by Yuri
Gorbachev."
THE SUNDAY TIMES (Singapore).
June 5, 1994.

"Yuri Gorbachev's Latest Works
Have Mythological Themes."
SINGAPORE TATLER.
June 1994.

Reyes, Carmina E.
"Yuri Gorbachev: What Sells is Not
the Name but His Paintings."
MANILA BULLETIN (Manila, Philippines).
June 20, 1994.

"Gorbachev the Artist."
PHILIPPINE TIMES JOURNAL
(Manila, Philippines).
June 1994.

J.G. Wilburn.
"Art Review: Absolutely Gorbachev."
BANGKOK POST (Bangkok, Thailand).
July 2, 1994.

Hutton, John.
"Arts: Gorbachev's Images
for His Perestroika."
THE WEST AUSTRALIAN
(Perth, Australia).
August 5, 1994.

Butcher, Adrienne.
"X Press Interview: Yuri Gorbachev."
X PRESS (Perth, Australia).
August 8, 1994.

Healy, Anthony.
"The Art of Diplomacy by Yuri
Gorbachev."
WINDOW (Hong Kong).
September 16, 1994.

"Tsar Gazing."
EVENING STANDARD (London).
November 9, 1994.

Bennett, Dave.
"A Taste for Primitive."
DAILY MAIL (London).
November 9, 1994.

Barker, Godfrey.
"Another Gorbachev in Picture."
DAILY TELEGRAPH (London).
November 11, 1994.

"San für den Maler Juri Gorbatschow:
Eva-Maria Hagen"
(Eva-Maria Hagen sings for Yuri
Gorbachev).
BERLIN ZEITUNG.
November 11, 1994.

"Gorbatschow stellt seine Bilder in Berlin
aus" (Gorbachev is still in Berlin).
BZ (Berlin).
November 23, 1994.

"Gorbatschow zeigt in Berlin seine schon-
sten Bilder" (Gorbachev Builds Beauty).
BERLINER KURIER.
November 24, 1994.

"Schneelandschaft mit Zwiebelturm"
(Landscape with horses).
DER TAGES SPIEGEL (Berlin).
December 12, 1994.

Sjostrom, Jan.
"Gorbachev Colors His World
With Paint."
PALM BEACH DAILY NEWS.
March 25, 1994.

"Kunstvoll naiv" (Naïve arts).
BERLIN MORGENPOST.
November 26, 1994.

"Blaue Hunde, lila Katzen und viel Gold"
(Blue dog, violet cat with gold).
NEWS DEUTSCHLAND (Berlin).
November 28, 1994.

"Juri Gorbaschow in der Galerie Miro"
(Yuri Gorbachev in Miro Gallery).
BERLINER MORGENPOST.
January 1, 1995.

"From Russia with Love."
HONG KONG TATLER.
January, 1995.

"Keramica je mimo politiky."
(Ceramics without politics).
PRAVDA (Slovakia).
January 10, 1995.

Doyle, Greg.
"The Arts: Gorbachev Holds
Exhibition."
JAKARTA POST.
January 29, 1995.

"Yuri Gorbachev Presents Naïve Art."
SINAR (Jakarta, Indonesia).
February, 1995.

"Artist Yuri Gorbachev."
FEMINA (Jakarta, Indonesia).
February, 1995.

"Personality: Yuri Gorbachev."
JAKARTA MAGAZINE.
February, 1995.

148

Klages, Karen E.
"Russian Unorthodox."
CHICAGO TRIBUNE.
June 4, 1995.

Musco, Ralph.
"The Rise of Another Gorbachev."
SUNSTORM FINE ART.
Spring 1995.

Goldberg, Carey.
"The Other Gorbachev."
THE NEW YORK TIMES.
August 27, 1995.

———. "The Other Gorbachev."
THE INTERNATIONAL HERALD
TRIBUNE.
August 31, 1995.

Hakanson Colby, Joy.
"Exhibit Review: Gorbachev's
Brush With Success."
DETROIT NEWS.
September 14, 1995.

"Russian Dressing."
DETROIT MONTHLY.
September 1995.

Batchan, Alexander.
"Rasskaz O Yuria New York Pokorivschem"
(Story about Yuri who wins in New York).
ESTET (Moscow).
November 1995.

YURI GORBACHEV: BALI SERIES.
Catalogue. Jakarta:
Mimi Ferzt Gallery. 1995.

Siddhartha, Amir.
"Yuri Gorbachev Transforms
Fantasies in Bali Series."
JAKARTA POST.
January 27, 1996.

Narayan, Parvathi Nayar.
"Peak Personality: Edged in Gilt."
THE PEAK (Singapore).
Spring 1996.

Carpenter, Bruce W., Konstantin K.
Kusminsky, and Amir Siddartha.
BALI ICONS BY YURI GORBACHEV.
Bali, Indonesia: Ganesha Gallery.
1996.

"Art and Culture Review: From
Russia with Love."
BALI KINI (Bali).
December 1996.

"Now You Know."
WASHINGTON POST.
January 17, 1997.

Ribut, Made.
"Bali Icon Exhibition."
BALI ECHO.
January 1997.

"Novostiy O Ludia: Yuri Gorbachev Vbellum
Dome" (Personality news: Yuri Gorbachev
in the White House).
MEDVED (Moscow).
March 1997.

"Seeing Red."
SUNDAY TELEGRAPH
(Sydney, Australia).
March 16, 1997.

"Coq Yuri Gorbachev Pocoril Ameriku"
(How Yuri Gorbachev conquered
America).
YEVGENY GOLUBOVSKY
(Odessa, Ukraine).
July 1997.

Callcott, John A.
"Yuri Gorbachev: Artist in the Family."
HORS LIGNE (Geneva).
Autumn 1997.

Raya, Julia.
"A Special Kind of Heaven: Yuri
Gorbachev."
BALI KINI (Bali, Indonesia).
December 1997.

"From Russia with Love."
WORLD MAGAZINE (Singapore).
December 1997.

Museum & Public Collections

Blackpool Museum of Art, England

Capital Hotel, London, England

Central Library, Oulu, Finland

China Club, Hong Kong

Donezk National Fine Arts Museum, Ukraine

Far Eastern Plaza Hotel, Taipai, Taiwan

Financial Club, Jakarta, Indonesia

5 Penn Plaza, CNN Building, New York

Hilton Hotel, Singapore

Hyatt Regency Hotel, Perth, Australia

Ilyaichevsk National Museum of Porcelain and Earthenware, Ukraine

Karuna Passage, Miro Gallery, Prague, Czech Republic

Kiev Republic Museum, Ukraine

Kremlin Museum, Novgorod, Russia

Louvre Museum, Paris, France

Merck Fink and Co. Bank, Berlin, Germany

Ministry of Culture of the Ukrainian SSR, Ukraine

Moscow Cultural Centre, Russia

Moscow Museum of Porcelain and Earthenware, Russia

Museum of Art, Duke University, Durham, North Carolina

Museum of Art, Glasgow, Scotland

Museum of Art, Marseilles, France

Museum of Art, Oulu, Finland

Museum of Art, Stockholm, Sweden

Museum of Fine Arts, Genoa, Italy

Museum of Fine Arts, Gerona, Spain

Museum Seni Rupa, Jakarta, Indonesia

Museum Universitas Pelita Harapan, Lippo Karawaci, Indonesia

National Art Museum of Penza, Russia

Odessa East West Museum, Ukraine

Odessa Literary Museum, Ukraine

Odessa National Gallery, Ukraine

Porcelain Museum, St. Petersburg, Russia

Regent Hotel, Jakarta, Indonesia

Rudana Museum, Bali, Indonesia

Russian Culture Foundation, Moscow

Seagram's Company Museum, Absolut Vodka Collection

Shangrila Hotel, Manila, Philippines

Stolichnaya Collection, Carillon Importers

United Nations, New York

Jane Voorhees Zimmerli Museum, Norton Dodge Collection, Rutgers University, New Brunswick, New Jersey

West Slovakia National Gallery, Koschitza, Slovakian Republic

Selected Private Collections

150

Rose Marie Jimenez de Arenas

Sheik Mohamed Ashmawi

Joop Ave

Mikhail Baryshnikov

Yvgeny Boldein

Former UN Secretary-General
Boutros Boutros-Ghali

Mr. and Mrs. Alan Breitman

Mr. and Mrs. Leo Breitman

Mr. and Mrs. Arthur Bricker

Emanuel Cherdak

Robert Chong

President and Mrs. Clinton

Mr. and Mrs. Johnnie Cochran

Valera Danchenko

Mr. and Mrs. Max Devere

Norton Dodge

Alexander Dolsky

Mr. and Mrs. Henry Dormann

Baroness Dunn DBE JP,
Hong Kong

Mr. and Mrs. Frankie duVille

Britt Ecklund

Philippine Vice President
Joseph Estrada

Sergei Federov

Alisa Freindlich

Mr. and Mrs. Harold Fried

Mikhail Gorbachev

Dr. Armand Hammer

Dr. Gabriela Hascakova

Stephen Haymes

Agus Irawan

Mr. and Mrs. Daniel Iskandar

Mr. and Mrs. Neil Jacobs

U.S. Senator James Jeffords

Robbie Johan

Karen Kekstadt

U.S. Senator Edward Kennedy

John A. Kerr

Felix Komarov

Peter Korompis

Vitaly B. Koutchouk, Russian Ambassador
to the Phillipines

Mr. and Mrs. Viktor Krupnich

Konstantin Kusminsky

Deddy Kusuma

Barry Landau

Nikolai N. Loginov, Russian Ambassador
to Singapore

Kay Malkmus

Paul J. Markowski

Serguei Martinenko

Mr. and Mrs. Barney McDermott

Dr. Molly Noonan

Mr. and Mrs. Chris Norton

Jan Ong

Mr. and Mrs. Christopher Patten

Alla Pugacheva

Astari Rajid

James Riady

Prince Viktor Y. Romanov

Michel Roux

Mr. and Mrs. Royal Rowe

Nyoman Rudana

Siti Hardijanti Rukmana

Hanni Saltzman

William Saroyan

Joyce Selander

Edouard Shevarnadze

Queen Sirikit, Thailand

Miro Smolek

Christine Sperber

Dr. Barbara Sullivan

Mr. and Mrs. James Tabalujian

David Tang

Princess Galyana Vadhana, Thailand

Mr. and Mrs. Bruce Verstandig

Roman Vichtuk

Dr. Barry Weintraub

Sukmawati Wijaya

Mr. and Mrs. Rich Winter

Yakov Yavno

Exhibitions

1977 – 1990
Exhibitions at major museums, cultural institutions, and galleries in the former USSR

1987 – 1989
Exhibitions throughout Finland; Prague, Czechoslovakia; Barcelona and Gerona, Spain; Genoa, Italy

1990
New York Viewing Room, New York, New York

Red Square Gallery, London, England

1991
L'Univers des Art Gallery, Marseilles, France

1992
Golden Autumn Auction, Sotheby's Auction House, Fisher Island, Florida

Russian Tea Room, New York, New York

Ashawag Hall, East Hampton, New York

International Fine Print Dealers Association Fair, Park Avenue Armory, New York, New York

Heidi Neuhoff Gallery, New York

1993
Mimi Ferzt Gallery, Hong Kong

Mimi Ferzt Gallery, China Club, charity auction to benefit children with Down's syndrome, Hong Kong

1994
Kenneth Raymond Gallery, Boca Raton, Florida

Kristal Gallery, Sugar Bush, Warren, Vermont

Michalski Galleries: Singapore; Manila, the Philippines; Bangkok, Thailand; Perth, Australia; Taipei, Taiwan

China Club, Hong Kong

Caldwell Snyder Gallery, San Francisco, California

Roy Miles Gallery, London, England

Miro Gallery, Berlin, Germany

1995
Financial Club, Jakarta, Indonesia

Koi Gallery, Jakarta, Indonesia

Merck Finck & Company Bank, Berlin, Germany

Art Miami, Caldwell Snyder Fine Art, Miami Beach, Florida

Caldwell Snyder Fine Art, New York, New York

Hong Kong Art Fair, Caldwell Snyder Fine Art, Hong Kong

Merrill Chase Galleries, Chicago, Illinois

Wagner Gallery, Sydney, Australia

Miro Gallery, Prague, Czech Republic

Europa Art Gallery, West Bloomfield, Michigan

Galerie Adrienne, San Francisco, California

1996
Mimi Ferzt Gallery, Regent Hotel, Jakarta, Indonesia

Gracie Lawrence Gallery, Delray Beach, Florida

Miro Gallery, Munich, Germany

Sierra Gallery, Lake Tahoe, California

Opus Gallery, Cleveland, Ohio

Europa Art Gallery, West Bloomfield, Michigan

Galerie Adrienne, San Francisco, California

Merrill Chase Gallery, Chicago, Illinois

1997
Ganesha Gallery, The Four Seasons Resort, Bali, Indonesia

Wagner Gallery, Sydney, Australia

Caitlyn Gallery, St. Louis, Missouri

Fine Art Auction benefiting National Children's Leukemia Foundation, Lincoln Center, New York, New York

Galerie Adrienne, San Francisco, California

Gateway Gallery, Vail, Colorado

Chabot Gallery, San Jose, California

Miro Gallery, Prague, Czech Republic

West Slovakia National Gallery, Koschitza, Slovakian Republic

1998
Ganesha Gallery, Four Seasons Resort, Bali, Indonesia

Gallery of Four Seasons Hotel, Singapore

Emerald City Fine Art, Seattle, Washington

Gateway Gallery, Vail, Colorado

Merrill Chase Galleries, Chicago, Illinois

Galerie Adrienne, San Francisco, California

Caitlyn Gallery, St. Louis, Missouri